THE SOVEREIGN ARTIST

Cover Design by Andrada Simion

The Sovereign Artist
Meditations on Lifestyle Design

VIZI ANDREI

viziandrei.com

Copyright © 2024 by Vizi Andrei

All rights reserved. No portion of this book may be reproduced in any form whatsoever without written permission in writing from the author.

Cover Design by Andrada Simion
Edited by Vizi Andrei
viziandrei.com

To my Mother and Father

In Memoir of my Lovely and Loveful Childhood

Contents

Preface
Economy of Truth . . . 9
The Architecture of this Book . . . 11
Investigation: Is Philosophy Dead? . . . 15
The Sovereign Artist Archetype . . . 21

Prologue
The Sicilian Dream . . . 25
The Sovereign Artist . . . 27

Appetizers . . . 31
Invitation to Slow Living . . . 35
How to Waste your Time . . . 41
The Art of Procrastination . . . 55
Book Shopping with Umberto Eco . . . 67
Sipping Wine with Plato & Da Vinci . . . 75
The Courage to Live a Simple Life . . . 85
Don't Forget your Dessert . . . 95

Epilogue
Declaration of Independence . . . 101
Recommended Readings . . . 113
Acknowledgments . . . 117

I don't feel like writing except in explosive states, in a climate of intense or abject feelings. Inspiration is simply a sudden spiritual imbalance I take advantage of.

I haven't written much in "moderate" frames of mind. I don't pick up my notebook when I'm *slightly* disgusted or *somewhat* euphoric. I pick up my notebook when I'm brimming with joy, vanity, guilt, or frustration.

VIZI ANDREI

PREFACE

Economy of Truth

OT LONG AGO, I wrote my first book called *Economy of Truth*—which is no longer available. It was an exciting project. It was an endeavor to find out who I am and who I want to be. I wrote it because I needed it. I wrote *Economy of Truth* because it's the book I wanted to read.

But—this is a big *but*—I made many mistakes. I was reluctant to seek feedback and advice. I rushed the entire process. The book came out poorly structured. I no longer resonate with the work I created. The scope, marketing, and promotion behind it were lacking in terms of style and elegance.

Despite all of these mistakes—*the book was quite successful.* Thousands of ladies and gentlemen bought it. The reviews were generally positive and constructive. And I constantly receive plenty of messages from people online asking me where they can buy my book from, even though I no longer talk about it online. *What's happening? Could this be serious?* This must be critical market feedback. The project was rather uncreative—yet people liked it. The demand was there. The demand *is* there.

This is why I decided to bring it back to life. I've been working on this project—at a leisurely pace and only when I felt inspired—for seven years in total. I refused to consider this "work" and, as a result, everything felt like play. I hope you'll enjoy reading it as much as I enjoyed writing it.

I doubt I will be satisfied with this book seven years from now. Perhaps all artists have the same relationship with their craft. The chances are, I will consider it immature or mediocre by then. Yet this time, with all its faults and omissions, I will leave this book as it is. I will resist "upgrading" it. As soon as I feel embarrassed by this book, I will start working on the next one. And I wish to keep the trend going.

VIZI ANDREI

Transylvania, Brașov
April, 2024

PREFACE
The Architecture of this Book

HE SOVEREIGN ARTIST is a collection of meditations on lifestyle design in the form of short essays and aphorisms. My ambition is to challenge you with a new philosophy of work and leisure—an avant-garde *dolce far niente*.

What is an aphorism? Aphorisms are crisp, well-decorated, rhetorical ideas distilled into a few words. They maximize utility while advancing or at least not degrading the truth. They turn valuable yet knotty lessons into vibrant intellectual structures. They're the poetry from the non-fiction section. Simply put, aphorisms foster an *economy of truth*.

Aphorisms are, by necessity, reductions of reality. Whenever you come across an aphorism that makes you grimace with dislike, don't test its universality—find out whether it's fun or practical. If a map takes you to your desired destination as smoothly as possible, it doesn't mean it's an accurate representation of reality. It doesn't show you everything. It only shows you what's useful.

THE ARCHITECTURE OF THIS BOOK

Think of aphorisms as you think of maps. They're maps of reality but *not* the reality; they make reality bearable. In other words, aphorisms are tools, not answers.

I've always been drawn to authors such as Chamfort, Nietzsche, Schopenhauer, Cioran, Taleb, and—probably my favorite—Nicolás Gómez Dávila. What I love about their writing is that they gift you all of their cheat codes without explaining them; they crystallize everything they know in a few words, lines, or paragraphs. Even their best essays rarely amount to five or six pages. This form of expression is seemingly lazy but profoundly difficult to reproduce.

Aphorists skip the conscious—and rather arduous—creative process and outsource everything to their hopefully reliable subconscious—they care about the outcome, the final product. They don't want to *create* the product; they only want to *ship* it. They don't want to *build;* they want to *sell*.

If you take a look at their lifestyles and routines, most aphorists share similar patterns. They allow themselves plenty of time for silence and boredom. They often take long walks or naps, read old books, sip wine, listen to music, and engage in various kinds of meditation. This is when the subconscious works really hard and takes care of the creative process. At some point, without

THE ARCHITECTURE OF THIS BOOK

notice, a decision is made: *the aphorism is ready to be packaged and delivered.*

All essays from this book are failed aphorisms which organically developed into divagations and some sort of pseudo-fiction. Although they're philosophical in nature, I'm no philosopher. I'm a *promoter* of philosophy.

To kick off my marketing campaign, allow me to draw your attention to an underrated modern tragedy...

PREFACE

Investigation: Is Philosophy Dead?

**LEGANCE BEING** alien to him, my professor enters the room wearing a whacky suit, ready to teach us...something. It's hard for me to pay attention, so I choose to daydream for a while—at first about nonsense, but then, as I stay firm in my decision not to follow his thread, I manage to scribble down some notes...that have nothing to do with his lecture. I can't tell exactly what he was trying to teach us, since it was that kind of information you forget seconds after taking the exam.

Most self-help books are nothing but kitsch philosophy... A consumerist form of "wisdom" and also a strange modern trend that doesn't seem to end soon... Terrible advice masquerading as "progressive" literature.

**OTH ACADEMICS** and the self-help industry killed philosophy. Academics managed to turn philosophy into the most boring subject on the planet; the self-help industry made philosophy

"accessible" by getting rid of the values, rigor, and erudition required to properly produce a work of philosophy.

The challenge is clear. *How can we bring philosophy back to life?* How can we turn this now dull, impractical, and at times degenerated subject, overly concerned with theoretical precision or linguistic debris, into something entertaining without destroying its architecture? Making philosophy fun is dangerous.

Ludwig Wittgenstein, the Austrian philosopher, brilliantly remarked that "a serious philosophical work could be written consisting entirely of jokes."

> *"When I was a child, I wanted to become a standup comedian. But then I studied philosophy. So I became the joke."* — Mahmoud Rasmi

This is not a call to turn philosophy into comedy but rather that any philosophical work could very well be an expression of play. Philosophy enjoys the right to entertain the mind. Paradoxically, if philosophers wish to be taken seriously, they must have the courage to sprinkle some joy over their intellectual exercises.*

---

* John Allen Paulos wrote an amazing book called *I Think, Therefore I Laugh*. He's the inspiration for this section.

Going back to my favorite author, what I picked up from Nicolás Gómez Dávila is a very fun way to write called *scholia*. I've been aware of this tactic for a long time—since I'm formally trained in law—but I was yet to get seduced by it until I discovered his work.

Scholia are comments and meditations that emerge thanks to a clear source such as an essay or a book. It's a note-taking exercise that teaches you to aim for an *economy of truth*. You're free to copy an idea; add further interpretation; or link it to another story or thought that was randomly triggered by an insight you just came across.

Hence a controversy arises—does this mean that this book is *not* original? Philosophically, this is a rather banal issue. Legally and ethically, it's likely fundamental.

My position is that—I'm 26 years old right now—young people can hardly be original artists or thinkers. They simply can't. Most of them can't be original since they're yet to garner adventures and challenges. And they're yet to reflect upon them —*this is critical.* Mircea Eliade wrote that "reflections make you original, not experiences per se." Indeed, there are many young people who don't lack experiences but their understanding. Their lives are bursting with adventures! They've traveled the world; seen things you can't even imagine. *The problem?* They're yet to nourish and milk these events. As soon as you have a conversation with them—despite their impressive portfolio—you realize they (we) don't know much. I've recently met someone my age who has been through a lot of difficulties early on in his life and now enjoys unlimited success; he's living like a rockstar. Yet he's spiritually and emotionally mundane. Eliade adds that "young people are very similar to Balkan musicians who try to reproduce songs they hear; they give the impression that they're original because they don't understand the source very well." **Originality is what happens when you steal ideas you don't understand and hence misinterpret.**

One should be able to swallow nuances: it's not that I think *like* others but *with* others. Think of Montaigne, Roger Scruton, Julius Evola, Chesterton, Umberto Eco, Nicolás Gómez Dávila, Emil Cioran, Mircea Eliade, Andrei Pleșu, Rory Sutherland, Alain de Botton, Nassim Taleb, Tim Ferriss, Robert Greene, Ryan Holiday, or Naval Ravikant. As a heuristic, anything from this book that's witty and clever, consider it their deed. Anything silly, consider it my fault.

And since we're talking about faults—note that, in this book, you will encounter a great deal of *repetition*. The same ideas are often conveyed through different angles. Many aphorisms and essays are thus complementary. Contrary to popular belief, this is *not* a stylistic flaw but an intended strategy designed to reinforce the most important parts of this book.

Repetitio est mater studiorum.

Now, let's discuss the title of this book; we must shortly get the party started. Grab a glass of (preferably red) wine.[†]

[†] Right now, I'm drinking one glass of *Merlot* & *Cabernet Franc* from Catleya. Some Romanian wines are highly underrated.

PREFACE

The Sovereign Artist Archetype

ET ME INTRODUCE you to my dear friend, Antisthenes. He was a famous Greek philosopher—an Athenian, although he was said not to be a legitimate Athenian. In his youth, he bravely fought in the battle of Tanagra, which led Socrates to believe that his genes are not pure. He argued that the son of two Athenians could not be so brave, as Athenians would rather theorize about courage than be courageous.*

As he became older, Antisthenes slowly left the battlefield behind. He got drawn to the study of ethics, logic, and literature. He became an accomplished orator and is credited with the authorship of over sixty titles.

Not far from Athens, there was a different man—a man respected by all, admired by many, loved by few, and matched by nobody. *His name conveys power yet humility:* Marcus Aurelius.

---

* Socrates was right: Antisthenes had a Thracian mother.

Marcus Aurelius was arguably the most competent Roman emperor that ever lived. In contrast with Antisthenes, he only wrote one book, globally known as *Meditations*.

While Antisthenes was studying, Marcus was on the battlefield, organizing his army. Or maybe he was training, wrestling with his comrades. Or maybe he was in his office, preparing his strategy for the next battle. While the professor was *teaching* philosophy, Marcus was *embodying* it. Marcus Aurelius wasn't only a king; he was also a philosopher—but, he first became a king and then a philosopher.

> **Good philosophers start with theory and end up with action. Great philosophers start with action and end up with theory.**

Plato famously said that "the world would only come right when kings become philosophers or when philosophers become kings." What does that mean?

Maybe what he meant by that was, Alain de Botton wrote, "if we want great ideas to become reality, we need to ally them with power." If we want wisdom to be impactful, we need the spiritual and artistic capacity of thoughtful thinkers to be united with the organizational and practical skills of powerful leaders.

THE SOVEREIGN ARTIST ARCHETYPE

I call this hybrid archetype *The Sovereign Artist.* Someone who combines erudition with risk-taking. Art with business. Meaning with purpose. An intellectual vagabond. A strategic rebel.

This book is a collection of *Greco-Roman* musings.

Please note that there's one central quality all *sovereign artists* share—which could be grasped only if we take a short trip to Catania, Sicily.

PROLOGUE

The Sicilian Dream

 T'S LATE MORNING and I'm walking the narrow streets of Catania, Sicily, together with my future wife. At some point, we decide to get a coffee and admire the scene. Even though it's an ordinary day in November—I recall it was Tuesday—the place permeates with attitude.

There are almost no tourists in sight. The architecture has a scruffy elegance. There's laundry hanging from the windows. Children are playing football. Four Sicilian middle-aged men, sitting on the table in front of their butcher, are talking loudly while eating some raw meat.

We finish our coffee to then move towards *Piazza del Duomo.* In the southwest corner of the square, there's an entertaining scene, full of singing salesmen. Shouting and gesticulating, they try to get the buyers' attention. There's fresh fish, seafood, fruit and veg stalls as well as cheese and mushrooms from the mountain villages around Etna. The area is wet and smelly.

The workday ends soon after we get there; people then gather at their favorite hangouts. We try to blend in with the locals, entering a taverna. We order *Involtini di Pesce Spada* and one bottle of wine.

> **In Sicily, I learned that even top managers working for large companies aren't impressive—no matter how much money they make. Among Sicilians, the goal is to be free and self-employed.**

The Sovereign Artist

 **ALENDAR SOVEREIGNTY:** Ability to grab coffee with friends whenever I want, play basketball on Tuesday, and work when most people travel and travel when most people work.*

Audience Sovereignty: Loyal (maybe digital) community that financially and critically supports my craft (hi there)—let's say that the magic number is 1000 members, but 100 people who care about your work is already impressive.†

 **HE POWER OF SELF-EMPLOYMENT:** You want to be neither the boss nor the employee. Neither the slave nor the master. I work *with* others but never *for* others. Freedom at all costs.

---

* Inspired by Paul Millerd.
† Inspired by Kevin Kelly.

The Sovereign Artist

Optionality: I have both *scalable* and *non-scalable* sources of income. This gives me safety and opportunity at the same time but also the freedom to set my prices according to the value that I deserve. I work largely online and mostly asynchronously with 3-9 clients that pay me predictably every month or so. In return, they receive my services: think of digital branding. These are my non-scalable projects, and it takes me roughly 1-2 weeks every month to take care of them. This gives me the peace to tinker with my scalable (and rather artistic) projects, such as this book or workshops and retreats about wine and philosophy in Transylvania and beyond.

**NERGY SOVEREIGNTY:** Ability to reject projects that would make me "rich" but drain me spiritually or morally. This is the hardest part. And it requires a lot of discipline and wisdom.

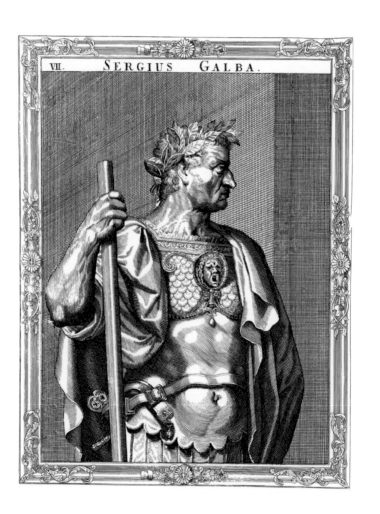

Appetizers

If you want a calm discussion about a hot topic, use an arsenal of cold phrases.

§

Kindness without truth comes across as flattery. Truth without kindness comes across as disrespect. Those who manage to find the sweet spot are the most persuasive.

§

If you can't appreciate science and religion at the same time, you understand neither.

§

A scholar that only trains in libraries is a soft thinker.

Love buys you time; reading helps you travel in time; play makes you forget about time; meditation teaches you to control time; and employment wastes your time.

§

Skepticism is the elegance of wisdom—but too much skepticism gets you drunk with impasse. **You want to be a *risk-taker* who *loves* uncertainty.**

Skepticism doesn't mean inaction but rather taking advantage of your doubts and questions—turning them into gold and profit.

§

The more offended you get, the more accurate the insult was.

§

Measure wisdom in risks taken, exposure to challenges, not years. A young wolf is wiser than an old dog.*

---

* Angela Jiang came up with a great heuristic: "Measure experience in exposure to shocks rather than years. By this measure, some of the young are old; some of the old are young; and some of the old are ancient."

My reason is simply a greedy lawyer hired by my guilty instincts, feelings, and values to prove them innocent. This lawyer is responsible to conserve and protect my identity from sudden changes. If I adjust my beliefs too quickly and too often—I risk going insane. I'm open-minded only in the sense that my mind is closed by openable windows.†

§

Don't waste time worrying about missing opportunities. Worry about not being in a place that attracts opportunities. If you are at the wrong bus station—every bus is the wrong bus.‡

§

Are your goals your own, or what you believe you should want? Are your dreams indeed authentic, or are they default ideals and prepackaged narratives designed by Hollywood, corporate advertising, and intensive social media sessions?

---

† And these windows have both shutters and curtains.
‡ Inspired by Sahil Lavingia & Mark Baker (@GuruAnaerobic via Twitter)

MEDITATIONS & APHORISMS

Invitation to Slow Living

You need silence to imagine a brighter future. Your mind requires boredom to carve out a destiny for yourself.

In a world full of distractions, boredom is no longer a mere "productivity hack"—it's one of the highest virtues.

§

We work hard and for long hours to reap the benefits that may only be enjoyed *occasionally*—during strict intervals or whenever they got scheduled in the (sometimes very distant) future:

We're waiting for the weekend, next vacation, or retirement!

This makes us end up with a chronic condition...

We constantly postpone the zest and will to love life.*

---

* Inspired by Andrei Pleșu.

One of the worst mistakes we make is believing that waking up in the morning is a right rather than a blessing. It may look like a strong claim; but it's a fragile gift. Only those who internalize this lesson in their life may finally become alive.

§

My best thoughts came to me through revelation—while taking long walks in the countryside, sipping wine and watching the sun go down, or doing nothing on my balcony other than admiring the view.

Almost nothing of value ever came to me sitting at my desk, through the instrument of reason. My office helps me be *productive*—that's indeed where the "hard" work gets done—but seldom *creative*.

Most ideas produced in my office are inevitably flawed, corrupted, and easy to dismantle.

§

The greatest accomplishment of a human, a busy primate, is to be able to spend hours and hours without doing anything.

ESSAY

Invitation to Slow Living

IT'S A SUNNY DAY in Bucharest; I'm flâneuring around my favorite neighborhood: Cotroceni. Lovely human-scaled architecture built during the interwar period—you can't help but wonder what vibe these streets used to boast 100 years ago.

As soon as you step out of the neighborhood, the scenery changes dramatically. You're forced to say goodbye to peace and beauty to enter a concrete jungle. High-rise communist blocks evenly separated by large boulevards await you. One minute ago you were in Paris or Istanbul; now you're in Moscow. There's no purgatory between these two worlds. I find this fascinating and unsettling at the same time.

Never in history was a capital city destroyed as much and as quickly during periods of peace as Bucharest was between 1980-1989. Many mixed-use neighborhoods featuring historic buildings—influenced by Byzantine and Western elements—but also houses in the vernacular got shattered by Mister Ceaușescu.

Some of them very nice; others quite banal yet still in harmony with the street and landscape. *How massive was the destruction?* To put things in perspective, in square meters, the equivalent of Venice. Cotroceni was supposed to be next. Luckily, this never happened as communism collapsed. And the plan (thank God) wasn't finished.

Something you immediately notice in Bucharest as an outsider—also in any other big cities—is that everyone is running somewhere. To catch the bus, metro, tram. Maybe they have a meeting. Or they're late for lunch. I saw one guy running to his Porsche (nice car indeed) to then get stuck in traffic.

I learned something ostensibly vapid yet incredibly valuable from Nassim Taleb: *don't be in a rush.* Resist running to be on schedule. This is an open invitation to *slow living.* Once you refuse to be in a rush, you will feel "the true elegance and aesthetics in behavior, a sense of being in control of your time, schedule, and life."

Constantly being in a rush is a declaration of slavery. This is no exaggeration; even if you're the CEO, the boss, the employer—if you sit at the top of a hierarchy—the truth is, you're not in control of your life. What I find ironic in big cities is that most people who're in a rush *look* rich or at least well off.

MEDITATIONS & APHORISMS

How to Waste your Time

Emil Cioran's favorite leisure activity was to travel by bicycle around France, exploring the countryside—always making sure to stop by the cemeteries he came across to meditate on death and the meaning of life.*

§

If you're not obsessed with tradition; if you don't understand it —you will never be able to innovate.

You won't come up with anything original if you don't take the time to study what's truly timeless and perennial.

You can't blossom if you're at war with your roots.

Your work will not last; it will likely be hollow and meaningless.

---

* Instead of reading yet another philosophy book, why don't you take a walk through a cemetery? H/T Mark Baker (@GuruAnaerobic via Twitter)

What doesn't allow you to live the way you want to live is the belief that you "have" to accomplish what you're "supposed" to do instead of following your genuine interests and curiosity.

I stole two rules from Naval Ravikant: "better bored than busy" and "only the unscheduled life is worth living."

The best strategy I use in order to stay consistently fulfilled is to bake boredom and silence into my life in a completely non-negotiable way.

I learned that, by constantly setting goals, drafting plans, and committing to plenty of different tasks—you slowly kill your soul. Too much structure turns you into a boring machine.

Once you learn to trust your curiosity—you're no longer the driver but the vehicle. Curiosity takes the lead, like a divine force. Being a slave to your curiosity paradoxically sets you free.

§

I write because that's what I do; not because that's what I want to do. There's no conscious decision or desire but rather an instinct or necessity.

You don't suffer from stress because you're doing stressful things; you suffer from stress because you allow yourself little to no time for silence and boredom. You suffer from stress because you're terrible at the art of doing nothing.†

You're in control of your life only if you can rest and relax without feeling any remorse.

§

I rest and relax because I love to rest and relax—not because leisure is something that helps me *recharge* to get ready for work. I don't relax to work; I work to relax.

Why would I optimize for labor?

§

To live well, don't look for *answers*. Learn to love the *questions*.

Life is much more about wonder, adventure, and reflection rather than evidence, order, and direction.

---

† Inspired by Ashwin Sharma.

During the week, I tend to take long walks and spend most of my time meditating in cozy cafés—I'm grateful that I live in a human-scaled town in Transylvania, brimming with colorful vernacular and baroque architecture, surrounded by nature.

My work seldom feels like work. It feels like play. Ironically, the more it feels like play, the better the results.

§

The difference between workaholics and slaves is largely psychological. Slaves are *forced* to work hard; workaholics are *programmed* to choose to work hard.

The alchemy lies in giving the victims a sense of independence about their decisions.

§

Logic, if used as the main instrument for thinking, frustrates the functions of the mind—it doesn't improve them.

Great ideas are the result of undirected curiosity, creativity, serendipity, and higher pleasures.

ESSAY

How to Waste your Time

I was reluctant to publish this essay as everything you're going to read is based on random notes (scholia) I took while reading the works of Emil Cioran, Mircea Eliade, Nicolás Gómez Dávila, and Aldous Huxley; they came up with brilliant remarks about the decline of leisure, rest, and entertainment. Accusing me of plagiarism wouldn't necessarily be a mistake. This essay is an attempt to structure all of these comments and hopefully morph them into something useful and coherent. I quote the authors when I directly stole their writing; however, when it comes to Eliade's work, please note that I translated most of his essays in English as they're largely available in Romanian and French. While translating his essays, I added extra context, interpretation, and clarification. The result is predictable: I ended up butchering the entire text and came up with novel thought exercises that are only mildly related to Eliade's genius. This doesn't mean that they're "original" but rather that attributing them to Eliade would be disrespectful to his legacy. The same rule applies to the other writers: my annotations give birth to divagations that, at times, have almost nothing to do with the original format in terms of substance and aesthetics.

HE "BEAUTY" about prioritizing leisure in your life is that you get to realize how degenerated leisure activities are today. We work so hard to the extent that, when we finally take a little break from work—we have no idea how to rest and relax.

Whenever we hear the word *"leisure"*—we think of watching Netflix, scrolling TikTok, or playing video games. Yet this definition is drastically misleading. Leisure historically meant freedom for social, creative, and intellectual activities. In Greek, leisure is rendered as *scholé*—this means school. The Romans had a similar word for this in Latin—*otium*—referring to reflection, contemplation, or the pursuit of academic interests.

Jesus used to go fishing with his disciples. Seneca wrote about how Cato loved to sip wine and reflect on the meaning of life. Emil Cioran, the most famous Transylvanian philosopher who spent most of his time in Paris, liked to relax by writing joyful letters to his friends and family. John Rockefeller used to take regular breaks from his notoriously demanding schedule to mill about in his garden. Benjamin Franklin's work sessions were broken up by periods of conversation, reading, and boredom.

Pure leisure paradoxically requires discipline, focus, and commitment, not an endless pursuit of dopamine.

My friend, Jash Dholani, surprised me with a few facts:

> Notice the *"fort"* in comfort. The Latin root of comfort means to fortify—to get stronger. **The original sense of comfort was rest that gets you ready for war.** Leisure must not be an escape from effort; it must be unavailable without effort. At royal weddings, theological debates were arranged as entertainment. Logicians debated God at Prince

Palatine's engagement. Aldous Huxley wrote that, in Elizabethan times, regular people "could be relied upon to break into complex musical acts" like madrigals or motets. Some people had to "exert their minds to an uncommon degree to entertain themselves."

We're barely able to identify any aristocracy today who prefers amusements that require some sort of social, creative, or intellectual effort, let alone regular people.

In 1927, Mircea Eliade was complaining about how young men in Bucharest "patch up their mediocre souls" with the latest issues of *La Nouvelle Revue Française* or *Insel Verlag*. May you be blessed to be surrounded by such mediocrity today!

Not long ago, recreation was a consequence of active collaboration between family members and neighbors. The goal of baking bread, my grandma used to tell me, was not to bake bread but to make friends. Italians—largely in the south—deserve their reputation: they still gather to play cards, sing, fish, or sip coffee and wine.

Pure leisure is closely related to the art of wasting your time. This is my favorite form of happiness. And also a divine search tool for wisdom. This kind of art has been long forgotten. And it's been forgotten because we no longer know how to take control of our free time. Eliade came up with a bitter observation in 1934. At the time he wrote this, maybe he exaggerated—yet today, his words hit home with the precision of an arrow finding its mark:

> **Never before have there been so many automated, mechanized, commoditized entertainment products as we "enjoy" today... Most if not all modern amusements are designed to dominate your free time and integrate it into fake leisure activities.**

Consider the cinema. You get tickets to a movie and agree to have your critical behavior dominated by the subject of the show for 2h and 23 minutes. Aldous Huxley came up with a harsh remark: *"Countless audiences passively soak in the same tepid bath of nonsense. No mental effort is demanded of them."* They only need to sit down, eat popcorn, and keep their eyes open. The entire planet goes out on Saturday to watch something a bunch of fellows from Hollywood put together.

Or think of football games. As I'm writing this essay, Real Madrid is soon to play against Manchester City. I'm a big fan of Real Madrid—I thus confess that I've just entered a contract to have my eyes, ears, and feelings controlled for 90 minutes starting at 9 PM CET tomorrow. Tough game. *Hala Madrid!*

Eliade joins the party yet again:

> This kind of entertainment doesn't give you any "free time" but rather takes it away. Mass-manufactured "leisure" activities turn you into a prisoner. The modern spirit boasts an oddly painful tendency to standardize even the most spontaneous human expressions. We globally agree to have "fun" based on the same rules, rhythm, and intensity.

Technology only makes things worse. Everyone of us now keeps a tiny supercomputer in our pockets that's ready to entertain us everywhere we go. We can have a little bit of "fun" whenever we want. Boredom is a myth; silence is a fairy tale.

These are the best possible conditions to keep artistic cultures dead. There can be no creativity without silence and boredom since the root of any creative undertaking lies in the ability to *waste your time* with elegance and style, without feeling guilty.

Think of all the people living in Tokyo, London, Dubai, New York, or Los Angeles. They have something "fun" to do available at all times. Are they ever able to spend time alone, in silence, meditating on random existential crises? Do they ever get bored?

HOW TO WASTE YOUR TIME

Paradoxically, only those who know how to waste their time are truly busy, productive, and hard-working.

I met a young man from Croatia who's been living in the US for the last five years or so; he told me he barely misses his country—he finds it boring, as there's "nothing to do"—and claims he can't see himself living anywhere else but in a city such as Chicago, New York, or Boston.

I can't deny the charming vibes of a couple of big cities in this world. And I can't deny that living in a big city does bring some benefits, especially when you're young—since your goal is to expose yourself to as many opportunities as possible. But if you dislike quiet, human-scaled places—you're simply disconnected from Nature.

The quality of your **leisure** *predicts the quality of your* **work.**

How many of us choose to work because our ambition springs from a boundless desire to manifest ourselves spiritually? How many of us start projects, not strictly as a result of financial considerations, but because they are genuine expressions of who we want to be? Are you able to identify five true artists, scholars, or scientists among us? Can you even name one polymath that's not dead? We work because we simply provide a service.

Just skim through Leonardo Da Vinci's notebooks; notice in what frame of mind he was, and how foreign this is from our "artist" models. Take a look at how obsessed Dostoevsky, Nietzsche, or Kafka used to be. Do you think they had a "job" or "hobby" or rather a mission to fulfill?

Are academics today organically interested in the subjects they claim to pursue, or do they simply narcotize their minds with the same set of concepts from 9-5, Monday-Friday to secure an ongoing employment? This is, of course, a rhetorical question.

The art of wasting your time doesn't translate into intellectual laziness or eternal vagabonding. It's about being open to wonder, adventure, miracle, and serendipity. It's about being comfortable with uncertainty.

"Creativity starts with an empty calendar," Naval Ravikant wrote, "and ends with a full one." You seldom live more gracefully than when you waste your time.

There's an intriguing concept I came across (thanks to Evan Armstrong, lead writer at Every) called *"afflatus"*—it comes from Latin and means a sudden rush of inspiration, seemingly from the divine or supernatural. Few experience this; probably because it's counter-intuitive. To get there, you don't have to "optimize" your work but prioritize leisure. You need *sacred* leisure. Knowledge workers today dream about achieving dozens of tasks every week. There's a relentless pursuit of optimization. Predictably, they often fail and end up being dissatisfied with the quality of their systems. Evan describes why this kind of thinking didn't serve him well:

> Self-improvement is great and productivity is wonderful, but something about this vein of thought feels off. When I try to follow this advice, I may temporarily get more stuff done, but it comes at the expense of my soul. I feel like an obsessive and compulsive lumberjack, hyper-focused on marginal improvements in my sawing technique—until one day, as I finish my labors, I realize I accidentally clear-cut the forest for the trees. **My success has happened because I've given myself *space* to ignore all the extra things I'm supposed to do so I can pursue *afflatus*.** I'm not advocating for a lifestyle of ease and no work. There are always late nights and sacrifices. What I'm arguing for is the cultivation of a state of being to allow for *afflatus* to occur.

MEDITATIONS & APHORISMS

The Art of Procrastination

Even Michalengelo would have trouble getting out of bed if he had nothing but a day of spreadsheets ahead.

It's impossible to imagine Leonardo da Vinci working for a corporation or being a government bureaucrat.

If your projects lack flavor and you have no skin in the game—your body will not produce energy. You will procrastinate.

Jash Dholani adds extra notes:

> Energy is simply the by-product of courage. Lethargy is the hint that somewhere, somehow, you made the coward's bargain. Great ambition appears out of nowhere in the face of great risks and great tasks.

No one yawns if they see a monster entering their room. *Find your monster.*

Show your anger when needed.

People need to know what irritates you and what doesn't.

But you want to stay *internally* calm.

Your anger is only a tool. Don't become its puppet.

§

Working *less* is not laziness.* Doing *less* meaningful work is not laziness. Laziness is enduring an existence you dislike.

Contrary to popular belief, working "hard" and being "busy" all the time is a form of laziness—lazy strategic thinking and management skills.†

---

* One rule I learned from Jim O'Shaughnessy—that I now apply in all contexts at work—is that you want to avoid busyness at all costs. Being busy must be so passé to the extent that you consider it a clear sign of failure; an outdated strategy to lie about your productivity. Maybe this rule sounds obvious. But the innovation lies in making it the constitution of your business; not a mere idea you consider every now and then.
† Rich Webster argued that working *hard* is, in fact, easier than working *less*. "If you want to work less, you have to focus. You have to build discipline. You have to delegate. And you have to prioritize rest." To work hard, you simply have to work hard.

Your "passion" emerges as a result of trial-and-error tinkering rather than predetermined desire or choice.

Contrary to popular belief, you don't have to aim at something.

Follow your curiosity and see what happens.

§

Artists who only study art happen to be clumsy artists; as well as philosophers who only read philosophy tend to be foolish philosophers.‡

You can't bring out the flavor of your mind if you're afraid to tackle subjects that lie outside of your professional or intellectual comfort zone.

§

Most people don't have an opinion on a lot of things.

Until they're asked about them!

---

‡ Inspired by Emil Cioran.

At which point, they decide to cobble together a viewpoint from half-remembered hearsay and other mental debris—sprinkling so much confidence on this makeshift opinion as though it were their latest dissertation.§

Steven Pressfield came up with a great diagnosis: **"The disease of our times is that we live on the surface. Our knowledge is a mile wide and an inch deep."** We're brimming with opinions not when we know 70% about 5 topics but rather when we "know" 7% about 50 topics. There's a fascinating paragraph in *Conspiracy* where the author, Ryan Holiday, describes how Peter Thiel leads a conversation:

> If someone asks him a question—about some controversial issue of the day—he doesn't simply react with an opinion or pluck a conclusion from nowhere. Instead, he prefaces it with *"I tend to believe"* or *"It's always this question of"* as if what he's about to tell you is simply capturing where his opinion falls while running a thought exercise… Everything gets punctuated with liberal pauses to consider what he's saying as he's saying it, as if he's always in the process of deciding what he thinks.

---

§ Inspired by Gurwinder Bhogal.

We're no longer to be judged by what we know, but rather by what we know we *don't* know.

Judge someone not by their knowledge, but by their level of awareness of its limits.

§

A life of endless optionality is a life devoid of responsibility—precisely what enables freedom. Freedom starts with optionality and materializes with commitment.¶

§

To win an argument, rely on logic.

To win in life, *question* logic.

If you're not willing to take some actions that don't make sense, having a mediocre life will make perfect sense.

¶ This is why starting a family doesn't "take away your freedom" (this is a modern idea I find disgusting) but rather *creates* it. It's liberating to finally be responsible for something greater than yourself.

ESSAY

The Art of Procrastination

 **OFTEN FEEL** the urge to do nothing but read books—ranging from extremely specific subjects (such as the history and culture of Transylvanian Saxons) to general works of philosophy (anything I can find by Montaigne, Julius Evola, or Roger Scruton) and finally a little bit of fiction by Umberto Eco, William Blacker, and Alain de Botton.

What I learned about myself is that my favorite type of books either have an epistolary character or are written in the form of journals and notebooks. The transparency you find in such works is simply unmatched! This is what I find seductive: I get access to virgin meditations and confessions.

Emil Cioran has written some of the best letters I've ever read to his friends and family. Mircea Eliade, his intellectual comrade, also assembled a few therapeutic journals—one toxic habit I have is that I thoroughly enjoy rereading the parts where he had the guts to attack thinkers such Freud or Tolstoy. Likewise, my bet is that we're unable to grasp the real value of Leonardo da Vinci's notebooks—it's a miracle that they survived in such great shape and condition.

It probably makes more sense to adopt a systematic research process and thus only choose to read books directly related to the main subject of my projects... I tried to do this at some point.

That was the plan. And here's how it worked out:

The books I expected to get the least output from (meaning: notes, comments, and insights useful for my artistic projects) turned out to be the most fruitful. And the books directly related to the themes of my work barely produced any dividends.

> ***The difference between "reading" and doing "research" is similar to the difference between "leisure" and "work"—you turn something playful and nourishing into a form of slavery and suffering.***

Consider this book. It's safe to say that I've been wasting so much time reading to delay the writing process. No debates here—this is indeed a form of procrastination! I tried to fight this in the beginning. Yet it felt more natural to give it a chance, to allow procrastination to be in the driver's seat and finish the job.

The result? What felt like leisure—and at times wasted time—turned into promising essays and aphorisms.

In hindsight, I worked hard; I read and wrote enough. The "problem" is that it felt like play. And I have a compelling argument to prove that: there were days when I spent 6-9 hours locked in my office, writing and reading unceasingly in a fasted state—I simply drank water and black coffee. The only way you can possibly enjoy such deep work sessions is when your work feels like play. Otherwise, if it feels like work, you have to rely on herculean levels of discipline to focus on something for so long... I thus want to take this chance to redefine *discipline*—or at least help upgrade its meaning—and turn it into a by-product of wild, undomesticated, undirected, and genuine curiosity rather than a conscious effort to "suffer" and delay gratification *ad infinitum*.

In *Antifragile*, the philosopher Nassim Taleb makes the confession that he uses procrastination as a filter for his writing. If he feels strong resistance to writing a certain section, he leaves it out as a service to his readers: ***"Why should they read something that I myself didn't want to write?"***

It took John Ronald Tolkien over 12 years to finish *The Lord of the Rings*. Since its publication, the book has gone on to sell around 150 million copies. It's now ranked as one of the bestselling books of all time. Could you even imagine working on a project for 12 years? What about 22?

Michel de Montaigne reportedly worked on polishing his most famous book, *The Complete Essays,* from 1570 until 1592. He was quick to start—but very slow to finish. His French comrade, Louis de Bonald, came up with a witty remark: "All that is to last is slow to grow."

Bill Gates, it seems, is also a "terrible" procrastinator. He often found himself putting off his university assignments to work on his business. That's how *Microsoft* was allegedly brought to life. He stopped completing his unnatural duties to work on more meaningful projects.

In *Mastery,* Robert Greene talks about the power of embracing slowness and procrastination:

> When it comes to creative endeavors, time is always relative. Whether your project takes months or years to complete, you will always experience a sense of impatience and a desire to get to the end. ***The single greatest action you can take for acquiring creative power is to reverse this natural impatience.*** You thus come to enjoy the slow cooking of your project, the organic growth that naturally takes place.

The longer you can allow your projects to absorb your mental energies, the richer they will become.

Instead of fighting procrastination as though it were an illness, maybe we should learn to understand its utility.

What we often call "procrastination" is far from a vice; this is a misconception that spoils creative thinking and intellectual serendipity. Procrastination is not a wicked phenomenon but a source of wisdom.

MEDITATIONS & APHORISMS

Book Shopping with Umberto Eco

Philosophers have questions. Scientists have theories.

Entrepreneurs have projects. Artists have obsessions.

And amateurs have *ideas.*

§

It's impossible to have a fun conversation with someone who, prior to the beginning of the discussion, already made an unconscious decision to disagree with whatever you're going to say or argue.

§

Good writers choose their words carefully.

Great writers let the words choose them.

Being antimodern doesn't mean *conservative* or *traditionalist.*

It has nothing to do with being nostalgic about the past. But it has nothing to do with nihilism, relativism, or knee-jerk contrarianism either.

Being antimodern means to be nostalgic about the future.

It's about reinventing tradition, bridging the gap between the sacred and the profane, sympathetically merging timeless truths with modern drama.

The goal is to be totally avant-garde yet cemented in tradition.

§

We read books to find out what we already know but find it hard to express. The *expression* of ideas, not ideas per se, is what we seek when reading books.

§

We *often* call "open-minded" those who agree with what we think or dislike what we dislike.

We *sometimes* call "open-minded" those who disagree with us the way we expect them to disagree.

We *seldom* call "open-minded" those who challenge our beliefs with unexpected views.

It's hard to recognize creativity if it doesn't fit the orthodox description for what creativity is supposed to look like.

§

Read books slowly, with periods of reflection and meditation.

If a book barely challenges you at the first read, you won't likely read it again. And books that are not worth rereading are not worth reading in the first place.

If you don't read old books, you must be insane!

There are hundreds of people who have spent years beating their heads against the wall trying to solve the same problems you're dealing with. And they all decided to distill their wisdom in the books they wrote... You can steal that hard-won knowledge in a few quiet afternoons!

The fact that knowledge is cumulative and you were born later than Machiavelli, Kafka, Dostoevsky, Sylvia Plath, George Eliot, or Ana Blandiana calls for an opportunity that can't be missed...

You need to read; and you need to read a lot!

§

To figure out if someone is truly smart, ask them a couple of questions about some "hot" topics; something that recently came up in the news or went viral on the Internet.

The more often they genuinely reply "I don't know"—the less informed they are—the smarter they are.

In the modern world, ignorance is a blessing.

If you regularly find yourself up to date to many of the latest trends, this is a sign to pause and reflect.

ESSAY

Book Shopping with Umberto Eco

**ASSIM TALEB** confessed in *The Black Swan* he got mesmerized by Umberto Eco's erudition. The Italian philosopher was part of a "small class of scholars who are encyclopedic, insightful, and nondull." His personal library boasts more than thirty thousand books. The way most visitors react when they see it is perhaps predictable: *"Wooow! What a huge library you have! How many of these books have you read?"*

To make sense of this, Taleb came up with a witty term called the *antilibrary*. What does that mean?

It seems that, the more you read, the more your library grows. But there's a difference in pace—you read 1 book; you get 3 more books. You read 2 books; you get 6 more books. Why?

People generally feel bad about the growing number of unread books on their shelves. **"I still have so many books to read!"** What they don't know is that this is a virtue masquerading as procrastination. Taleb wrote: "Unread books are far more valuable than read ones; a private library is not an ego-boosting appendage but a research tool."

Indeed, the more you read, the more your curiosity grows. Hence you get more books. This means that the more you learn, the more you don't know, as the number of unread books on your shelves keeps growing and growing.

> *Even if you "read" all of the books from your library, it doesn't mean much. The beauty of reading is about rereading. The beauty of reading is about the actions you take and all of the reflections that get triggered thanks to the material in front of you.*

But there's another subtle nuance: the more you learn, the more you know how much you don't know. Your intellectual humility is getting stronger, as you're perfectly aware how ignorant you're since there's so much you're yet to discover! Your antilibrary is a constant reminder about both your limits of knowledge and ongoing curiosity.

MEDITATIONS & APHORISMS

Sipping Wine with Plato & Da Vinci

The human mind doesn't seek truth and accuracy.

Our minds didn't evolve to be *scientific* tools; they evolved to be *survival* tools.

Mother Nature didn't design them to be truthseekers.

She designed them to be *useful* for our mental, social, and emotional fitness.

§

Dare to build a vagabond intelligence.

Be a strategic rebel.

The education system teaches us to be specialists; but the real world is whispering that we need generalists and polymaths.

In 2002, Daniel Kahneman was awarded the Nobel Prize for Economics; although he's a psychologist. The Wright brothers are credited with inventing, building, and flying the world's first successful airplane; but they were not aeronautical engineers. Stoicism—arguably the most famous school of philosophy—was not founded by a scholar, but by a merchant, Zeno of Citium.

To innovate, as Arthur Schopenhauer put it, "the task is not so much to see what nobody else has seen but to think what nobody else has thought about that which everybody sees."

You want to enjoy a helicopter view over various subjects while having the capacity to land anywhere. You want to be able to bring in freshness, reject consensus, and reveal blind spots.

§

Discipline and creativity are impossible without curiosity.

Those who fail to get creative or build discipline don't know where to shop.

Creativity and discipline are not primary products; they're the by-products of genuine curiosity.

Curiosity gives work meaning and direction, which in turn give creativity and discipline a reason to show up.

Whenever you struggle to build habits or get excited,

Follow your curiosity and see what happens.

§

School is a game—to succeed, there are some rules you have to follow. *Life* means wilderness—there are no rules; it's all about survival. One habitat is predictable and organized; the other is complex and uncertain.

Dear student,

As soon as you leave school, get ready to exchange obedience with curiosity, logic with psychology, risk-management with risk-taking, and, above all, lecture with adventure.

§

You're free if and only if you failed to make the transition from the playground to the workplace.

You're free if and only if you seldom think about work during the hours not officially spent working—and when you do, your thoughts stir excitement, not anxiety.

§

You're free if and only if you love challenges, difficult tasks, and uncertainty—burdens that crush others are, for you, a form of recreation and asceticism. You hate safety and comfort.

§

I'm convinced that the best things in life are:

Red wine, honey, Croatian olive oil, being self-employed, love, old books, the Bialetti Moka pot, sunsets, and living in a neighborhood that wasn't planned by modernist architects.

Anything else is strictly unnecessary.

ESSAY

Sipping Wine with Plato & Da Vinci

My goal with this essay is not to downplay the risks of alcohol or make fun of people who got addicted to this substance. My grandfather died because of alcohol; and, sadly, quite a few people from my family also struggle with this addiction. This is indeed a widespread problem in Romania but also across the Balkans. I'm not declaring this to ask for sympathy or affection but to make you understand that I'm aware of how destructive alcohol can be. Please note that this essay is dedicated to wine and wine only and not to alcohol in general.

**LATO FAMOUSLY** said that "nothing more excellent or valuable than wine was ever granted by the gods to mankind." Is he wrong? Was he drunk when he said this? People who don't drink alcohol may get offended by this. People who drink too much alcohol—or have a history where they used to drink too much alcohol—may get offended by this too. I'm not interested in discussing whether wine is good or not. I'm certain this has nothing to do with wine per se. I'm only interested to find out *how* to drink it.

To do that, since we've already mentioned Plato, it's convenient to take a closer look at the Ancient Greeks. The best experiment they carried out was, like many things in life, counterintuitive.

This experiment, notable as the title of a work by Plato, is the underrated symposium—which is, in essence, a drinking party with clear rules and guidelines.

Roger Scruton came up with a great description:

> The symposium would invite Dionysus, god of wine, into a ceremonial precinct. Guests, garlanded with flowers, would recline two to a couch, propped on their left arm, with food on low tables before them. Manners, gestures, and words were as strictly controlled as at the Japanese tea ceremony; everyone was allowed to speak, recite, or sing, so that conversation remained always general.

It may be useful to consider that Leonardo da Vinci, Epicurus, Cato, Montaigne, and even Kant were great lovers of wine.

If cutting out alcohol has been a "game changer" for you— you likely (used to) drink the wrong alcohol in the wrong quantities with the wrong people for the wrong reasons and in the wrong contexts.

The great hero, Odysseus, shares his views on alcohol with a farmer, arguing that he indulges in wine so he can "dance, sing at the top of my lungs, and laugh like a fool!" There's a clear pattern here. Odysseus doesn't drink wine to drown his sorrows. He drinks so he can *dance, sing, and laugh*. He drinks to heighten his soul! He drinks in order to celebrate life.*

Roger Scruton adds an extra note:

> Of course we're aware of the medical opinion that a daily glass of wine is good for one's health; and also with the rival opinion that drinking more is not healthy. This is not unimportant—but as long as this is detached from the symposium culture, it doesn't make much of a difference. **Most people no longer have an arsenal of topics, books, poems, songs, and ideas with which to entertain one another in their cups. They drink to fill the moral vacuum generated by their culture.** And while we're familiar with the side-effects of drinking on an empty stomach, we're now witnessing the far worse effects of drinking on an empty mind.†

If you still want to insist that drinking wine is a vice, let's take a brief detour to the Ottoman shisha or hookah. My observation is

---

* My friend, Yago—@projectimpero via Instagram—deserves credit here.
† I once again encourage you to try my favorite Romanian wine: check out *Epopée by Catleya*. Both white and red. Drink it wisely. This essay is not sponsored by them; I simply love their wine.

that the greatest difference between smoking cigarettes and shisha is that consuming the latter entails some sort of pseudo-ritual while the former is a banal, mundane activity.

If you want to smoke shisha, there's a set of customs you need to abide by. You make a conscious decision to meet up with your friends in a specific place; you get some tea and never alcohol—the rule is simple: you're allowed only one single vice. Namely, the vice you came for. You never combine vices. I have a friend from Istanbul who's fed up with Russian tourists smoking shisha and drinking vodka at the same time; he has a point though: *Russians, vodka, and shisha* sounds like a terrible combination. And, finally, the experience requires thoughtful preparation. When the shisha is ready, you acknowledge its presence; a beautiful device that catches your attention. It's a special event. In contrast, cigarettes—first of all, they taste like crap—are all too convenient, too easy to get and consume. They're designed to make you addicted; smoking cigarettes is a habit that can be picked up anytime and anywhere. As Thomas Jefferson was surely right to argue that "wine is the best antidote to whiskey," my friends from Istanbul have the right to argue that "shisha is the best antidote to cigarettes."

Similarly, the symposium Plato wrote about entails only one "vice" and a ritual that needs to be respected. The greatest revenge against a culture that doesn't know how to drink alcohol is not to give up on it altogether and "go sober" but learn how to integrate it into a lifestyle packed with love, friendship, prudence, and philosophy. One rule I have is that a good wine should never be enjoyed alone; and it must always be accompanied by a good topic.

At the risk of getting canceled, my position is that if you truly enjoy wine—*then enjoy it!* Guilt is unnecessary. And note that prudence and pleasure are best friends, not enemies. This is not a medical opinion; this is for the soul. The problem is not that you drink (too much?) wine. The problem is that you make the same mistake both the hedonist and the abstainer make: you regard wine as a drug. The problem is that you've invested no ritual, ceremony, or genuine appreciation into this otherwise sacred drink—only aristocrats of the soul understand that this approach is not "elitist" but functional.

Roger Scruton is invited yet again to speak and end this essay in exactly the same fashion as Odysseus spoke to the farmer:

> *Wine—drunk in moderation at the right time, in the right place, and the right company—is the path to meditation, peace, joy, and philosophy.*

MEDITATIONS & APHORISMS

The Courage to Live a Simple Life

Measure wealth in love, freedom, and integrity rather than money, comfort, and material possessions.

By thinking all the time about money, you lose all the spiritual advantages of self-sufficiency.

Learn to be happy before you get rich.

§

We give up happiness to achieve success.*

We trade what we want—freedom and peace—so we can get rich in order to enjoy...freedom and peace. We give up our time to make money in order to have more time when we'll have "enough" money.

---

* Inspired by Chris Williamson.

"Desire is a contract you make with yourself," Naval Ravikant wrote, "to be unhappy until you get what you want."

I just came back from a short trip to Puglia; for some reason I enjoyed it more than Sicily. What I learned from Southern Italians is not how to romanticize poverty but that it takes very little to be happy. They have mastered the elegance of being wealthy without necessarily being rich.

The leap from making money to "pay your bills" to making money to "buy your freedom" is not so much about money but lifestyle design.

Paul Millerd, the author of *The Pathless Path*, believes this leap requires a "psychological shift in terms of how you see the world." There are plenty of people who earn millions of dollars that are unable to make the shift.

§

Extraordinary people lead *ordinary* lives.

Contrary to popular belief, there's nothing more complex, meaningful, and difficult to build than a simple life.

Look at the people further along the path in your field.

Are they who you want to be?

If the answer is NO,

You need to reconsider your career choices.

"I got out of the rat race," Daniel Vassallo wrote, "when I looked around me and realized that even the winners are miserable."

§

I find it baffling that—to improve their lifestyle—more and more people simply aim for scale. They want a *bigger* house. A *bigger* car. A *bigger* income. There's little consideration for qualitative aspects.

The obsession with bigness is profoundly American. Americans prefer way bigger houses and cars than Europeans—but the average American isn't necessarily happier or healthier.

The trick to a better life is to aim for things you can't measure with numbers. Beauty. Elegance. Peace. Love. Friendship.

Desiring your car or house to be bigger is not the problem. Desiring your car or house to only be bigger is the problem. Fetishizing bigness is the problem.

§

"You don't get any work done," Mark Baker wrote, "by being around people all the time."[†]

Emil Cioran complained in his letters to his brother about having too many friends in Paris. He was too busy to write. He liked to flee to Dieppe, a small town and fishing port on the Normandy coast of northern France, every time he couldn't focus properly.

To be able to finish *The Last Supper,* Leonardo da Vinci got up early every morning to arrive at the monastery so he could be alone, in silence, with his own thoughts and feelings.

Michel de Montaigne found intellectual refuge in his private library—which was located in the southern tower of his chateau.

[†] @GuruAnaerobic via Twitter.

When they were quarantined because of pandemic outbreaks, Shakespeare wrote King Lear; Newton invented calculus, developed his theory on optics, and formulated the laws of motion and gravity.

To discover that sense of sacredness at work, you need to give yourself *space* and *time* to be alone. Periods of isolation can paradoxically be liberating. "It's difficult to idealize yourself," Ryan Holiday wrote, "if you're never by yourself."

ESSAY

The Courage to Live a Simple Life

**AVING ANALYZED** a local shop owner, my mind got clear. She often wakes up around 5:00 AM, drinks a cup of coffee, prepares breakfast for her children, cleans up the house just enough to keep it in reasonable order, and goes to work around 7:30 AM... She's been doing her job responsibly and cheerfully since she was a very young lady; she managed to maintain a good-enough relationship with her husband over many years despite periods of extreme difficulty; and even though she doesn't come from a rich and supportive family, she's been keeping her small business alive for almost a decade, invariably defying the corrupt, disgusting Romanian tax authorities that have tried to close it down multiple times.

Surveying my own life, I realized that I fall short of her, my power of handling daily life not being such. Although anyone has troubles—at home, at work, or inescapably existential—and she is no exception, she confronts them with great diligence and inner strength. The alchemy may lie in developing strong respect for the often unpleasant randomness of daily life. She's a warrior invisible to the modern eye... She doesn't fit the standard definition for what courage is supposed to look like. Courage for her is a habit, not a once-in-a-lifetime remarkable act. We are blind to the nuances of courage because we are brought up to only attribute it to the acts of a few historical figures.

> ***Courage is much more about acting well in our daily challenges rather than extraordinary circumstances.***

Many kings, queens, generals, and soldiers deserve merits for acting heroically throughout history. There's a strong reason to admire their distinguished actions. Yet those who crafted the art of living—of coping with their daily challenges in a calm, sustained, and cheerful manner—deserve equal admiration, respect, and prestige.

There's immense skill involved in doing a fair business, raising your children to be reasonable adults, taking care of your garden, or keeping your house clean and tidy—in doing all of these while staying sane, joyful, and healthy.

"Ordinary life is heroic in its own way," Alain de Botton argues, "because ordinary things are far from easy to manage." It's true that not any ordinary act is courageous. But there are many which we tend to ignore that are so. These activities are impatiently waiting to be addressed and adopted in order to teach everyone what courage looks like on a daily basis.

There is much to learn from our lives if we decide to put on the right glasses and see that many of our ordinary activities hold, in fact, extraordinary qualities.

MEDITATIONS & APHORISMS

Don't Forget your Dessert

If you win an argument, you are not the winner.

The winner is the truth.

Lead the argument by order and style—then you're the winner!

A good discussion feels more like an elegant dance rather than a victorious battle.

§

The road to job security is paved with quicksand.

It seems safe and smooth on the surface, but the risks are hidden under the road.

In your career, you don't want to choose any road—but to find your own way through the wild.

If you always want to be "rational"—you can't be dangerous.

You're weak—because, by definition, you're predictable.

§

What does your ideal day look like?

Most people love to set "big" goals for the future…

But they fail to seize the present moment.

Instead of thinking at the macro level, begin by designing your perfect day. Once you're able to live 200+ such days per year, you're rich—even though you aren't rich.

§

Create a few stories worth telling your grandkids someday.*

Spend time in nature for a few days. Eat like a caveman. Travel only by bike. Find an old, traditional, non-touristic village and

---

* H/T Sahil Bloom.

live there for a few weeks. Talk to the locals. Help them out with their chores. Drink as they do. Party as they do.

Figure out what scares and inspires you at the same time.

Outside-the-box thinking requires outside-the-box living.

§

Romanians get excited if the train arrives on time. Austrians deem such an "event" *implicit*. What some believe to be a trivial circumstance, is for others a festival.[†]

§

Try to live far below your means for at least one month and watch how you're slowly learning what freedom tastes like.

§

The more you overthink a problem, the larger the debt your actions have to pay.

[†] Andrei Pleșu came up with a very similar thought; I only adapted it.

To understand both how fortunate and ungrateful you are, compare what "suffering" means to you with what it used to mean to your ancestors.

§

A generous act is generous only if you intend to get nothing out of it, not even a positive feeling. Experiencing satisfaction after the act should be a natural side-effect, not a conscious objective.

§

Progress: we're destroying natural landscapes, cultural heritages, and historical sceneries to build fantastic roads so we can drive faster than ever and go…nowhere.

§

We often discuss issues such as pollution, poverty, or corruption from a *global* perspective; yet we fail to consider them *locally*—in our city, neighborhood, or even family. We're thus trained to be irresponsible: the more we think and talk about problems we can't control—the more virtuous we feel but—the more we neglect the problems which are in our control.

Good marriages are bittersweet.

They need both kindness *and* honesty; privacy *and* intimacy; adventure *and* pragmatism; forgiveness *and* respect; arguments *and* empathy.

§

Those who argue to win arguments always lose them; even when they win them.

§

What we often call "rationality" is simply undetected rhetoric.

§

You're a fool not when you can't speak well on a given topic; you're a fool when you fail to remain silent.

EPILOGUE

Declaration of Independence

HEN I GRADUATED from law school, I made a promise to myself: "If you ever get employed, make sure it's only temporary—once you get too comfortable, you'll get trapped like a fly on a spiderweb." Luckily, I never got employed. Not even for one single day. I consider this the greatest success of my career so far.

I don't come from "rich" parents—although I'm immensely grateful for the rich education they gave me. I don't have any extraordinary talents; and I never took any dumb risk to start an overambitious business. I built everything organically, from the bottom up, in a world—the Information Age—that allows me to take plenty of small risks, place wise bets, and tinker or experiment with many different projects. I enjoy the freedom to make mistakes without being harmed by them.

My business model is (very) simple: I want to be able to take long walks, sip wine with my friends and fiancée, and play basketball on a random Tuesday at noon without asking for permission.

DECLARATION OF INDEPENDENCE

The goal is to build a lifestyle where I can take 200+ days off every year without getting lucky.

To figure out what I want, I didn't dream about building the "perfect" career. I started by defining my worst career nightmare. The first step toward learning what you want is being very specific about what you hate. And my worst career nightmare either means working in a corporate setting or becoming an overworked entrepreneur.

Nietzsche famously wrote that precisely when young people are ready to be sent out into the wild, they're instead put into "safe" jobs and positions.

I used to get anxious when I visualized myself working for a corporation. That's why I took action and decided to do something about my future. If you get similarly anxious—that's feedback. It's a signal to change something about your life.

In the first year of university, I started figuring out how I can build a service on the Internet revolving around my skills and interests. When I graduated from law school, I already had a few clients I was working with and a few projects or gigs that were profitable enough so that I could pay my rent and spend my time on my own terms. I wasn't earning a lot; but I was free.

DECLARATION OF INDEPENDENCE

I was self-sufficient. Plenty of my former colleagues were earning much, much more than I was. Being free is not always sunshine and roses—but you're free.*

Redefine work as a collection of projects, income streams, and experiments rather than one "safe" 9-5 contract or overambitious business.

I own a small branding agency (I only have 3-9 clients I work with); I host webinars about wine and philosophy; I run an online program about entrepreneurship in the Information Age; and I'm writing books in public.†

Working for yourself is obviously more challenging than 9-5 employment. It's hard to make the transition; for starters, you have to give up all of the benefits employment brings. Think of job security; maybe you get a company car; you don't have any

---

* My friend, Mark Baker (@GuruAnaerobic via Twitter) deserves credit here. One extra note: there are, largely, two types of stereotypes on the Internet who get massive attention. On the one hand, we have the crypto guy, the digital "entrepreneur" who solely makes money by teaching others how to make money. On the other hand, we have the corporate employee who claims to be "satisfied" with their banal career trajectory and shows others how to be happy too. Being employed is fine and can often be smart—as long as it's temporary. To escape the rat race, you have to be authentic; to design an original version of success. See *the Barbell Strategy* by Nassim Taleb.
† This is the first! Already working on the next one.

skin in the game (no risk if the company starts struggling or may go bankrupt); and you don't "feel" taxes: you don't have to (consciously) pay any.‡

I don't want to be a well-paid corporate employee for the same reason I don't want to be a well-fed lion in a zoo... If you got offended by this rather innocent declaration of independence, *ask yourself why.*

You don't have to build a traditional business—being an independent contractor already brings way more dignity and self-esteem. Or you can be a freelancer, creator, solopreneur, or minimalist entrepreneur. This is the subtle nuance plenty of people can't see. You no longer have to go all in. The Information Age has massively broadened the artistic and entrepreneurial possibilities. The risk is suddenly limited; but the upside stays unlimited.

Traditional entrepreneurship isn't for everyone—but there are other ways to take risks. Building something that can stand on its

---

‡ Paul Skallas (the Lindy Man) came up with a great observation. Throughout history, there were quite a few revolts against tax collectors. This doesn't happen as often anymore. Why? Maybe this is because people don't "feel" taxes today. They're taken out of your salary automatically. Only people who own small businesses—and pay manually—are obsessed with taxes.

own builds confidence. **Desiring full-time employment *ad infinitum* has nothing to do with "stability"—that's an illusion. You're, in fact, fragile.** You could build a few quasi-entrepreneurial and artistic projects that, combined, are far more "secure" than any 9-5 contract.§

One of the worst things I would hate to tell my grandchildren when I grow old is that I've stayed in a well-paid, comfortable job position my entire life doing nothing but sending emails and taking care of endless spreadsheets—waiting for my paycheck to predictably hit my bank account every month or so. It may sound like a gift. But it's a curse. "The problem isn't being on a steady salary," Nassim Taleb wrote, "the problem is enjoying it."

Risk-taking, starting a business; investing time, energy, hopes, and money—this is a virtue.¶

Be proud if you're building artistic or entrepreneurial projects. Even though you're not rich. You're entitled to be a tad arrogant. You have skin in the game. *Risk-takers build the world; and most employees benefit from it.*

---

§ See: *The End of Jobs* by Taylor Pearson.
¶ As long as it's not illegal or unethical. As long as it's not a ponzi scheme, MLM, or doesn't make money by teaching other people (generally young men fall prey to this) how to make money.

Notice

You may wonder—or maybe you're not; that's fine too—what's up with the four figures (illustrations) from this book that seem to have nothing to do with the content. They're not random. Recall that I'm already working on my next book. They give you a subtle teaser.

They're all archetypes. I used them to help you mildly rediscover mythology—these figures were meant to establish harmony within this book; to evenly infuse it with the *Sovereign Artist* wit and spirit. After all, myths, traditions, and symbols have nourished civilizations for millennia to come. My ambition is to reinvent these; and unapologetically integrate them into a contemporary form of writing that is neither progressive nor conservative but fundamentally *antimodern.*

Thank you for reading my book.

Artists who rely too much on systems, models, templates, methods, and frameworks lack spiritual passion.

As soon as your reason becomes the CEO of your projects—instead of being just another employee—your inspiration will get fired. Your work will lack energy, wit, and depth.

Artists who mastered the elegance of taking action when inspiration strikes—and of educating inspiration to show up predictably and generously—also boast an arsenal of systems, templates, and frameworks. Yet these are not the guardians of their craft; they're simply some casual friends.

To be continued...

Confession

Most of my writings are the product of a few fleeting moments of clarity and creativity; they only represent some snapshots of who I am. Besides these snapshots, I like to spend my days pushing doors that should be pulled, parking my car poorly, and often being socially awkward.

Recommended Readings

- Alchemy: The Surprising Power of Ideas that Don't Make Sense *by Rory Sutherland*
- Along the Enchanted Way: A Story of Love and Life in Romania *by William Blacker*
- Antifragile: Things That Gain from Disorder *by Nassim Nicholas Taleb*
- Brave New World *by Aldous Huxley*
- Figuring *by Maria Popova*
- Green Philosophy: How to Think Seriously About the Planet *by Roger Scruton*
- I Drink Therefore I Am: A Philosopher's Guide to Wine *by Roger Scruton*
- I Think Therefore I Laugh: The Flip Side of Philosophy *by John Allen Paulos*
- Mastery *by Robert Greene*
- Man and His Symbols *by Carl Gustav Jung*
- Men Among the Ruins: Post-War Reflections of a Radical Traditionalist *by Julius Evola*
- Notebooks *by Leonardo da Vinci*
- On the Heights of Despair *by Emil Cioran*
- Orthodoxy *by G. K. Chesterton*

Recommended Readings

- Patterns in Comparative Religion *by Mircea Eliade*
- Ride the Tiger: A Survival Manual for the Aristocrats of the Soul *by Julius Evola*
- Revolt Against the Modern World *by Julius Evola*
- Seeing like a State: How Certain Schemes to Improve the Human Condition Have Failed *by James C. Scott*
- Selective Breeding and the Birth of Philosophy *by Costin Vlad Alamariu*
- Skin in the Game: Hidden Asymmetries in Daily Life *by Nassim Nicholas Taleb*
- Small is Beautiful: Economics as if People Mattered *by E. F. Schumacher*
- The Art of Travel *by Alain de Botton*
- The Authentic Reactionary *by Nicolás Gómez Dávila*
- The Basic Laws of Human Stupidity *by Carlo M. Cipolla*
- The Bed of Procrustes *by Nassim Nicholas Taleb*
- The Biggest Bluff *by Maria Konnikova*
- The Complete Essays *by Michel de Montaigne*
- The Face of God: The Gifford Lectures *by Roger Scruton*
- The Fall of Spirituality: The Corruption of Tradition in the Modern World *by Julius Evola*

Recommended Readings

- The Hermetic Tradition: Symbols and Teachings of the Royal Art *by Julius Evola*
- The Masks of God: Primitive Mythology *by Joseph Campbell*
- The Minimalist Entrepreneur *by Sahil Lavingia*
- The Myth of the Eternal Return: Cosmos and History *by Mircea Eliade*
- The Name of the Rose *by Umberto Eco*
- The Pathless Path: Imagining a New Story For Work and Life *by Paul Millerd*
- The Power of Myth *by Joseph Campbell*
- The Sacred and The Profane: The Nature of Religion *by Mircea Eliade*
- The Trouble with Being Born *by Emil Cioran*
- The Tyranny of Experts: Economists, Dictators, and the Forgotten Rights of the Poor *by William Easterly*
- Thinking Like a Lawyer *by Frederick F. Schauer*
- What's Wrong with the World *by G. K. Chesterton*
- Yoga: Immortality and Freedom *by Mircea Eliade*

Acknowledgements

I'm a guilty man. Many of you will credit me for the ideas from this book. The truth is, as mentioned before, they were inspired by people way smarter and way more successful than I am. So, please keep in mind—whatever you found valuable, consider it their product; whatever you found silly, consider it my fault.

I want to thank my future wife, Geanina, who was a dedicated editor and reader of this book and for always believing in this project even when I felt it makes no sense to finish it. I want to thank my parents for their constant support and for never discouraging me from pursuing unorthodox goals. I want to thank Larry Sanger for reviewing *Economy of Truth* (the book this book is based on which is no longer available; check out the Preface) a few years ago. Although he's one of the most critical people I met—it makes sense; he's the co-founder of Wikipedia and has a PhD in Philosophy—he left a very kind and positive review. You can only imagine how much this boosted my confidence. Finally, I want to thank Chris Williamson, Abe Wolke, Naval Ravikant, Jim O'Shaughnessy, Jash Dholani, Tiberiu Cojocaru, Andrei Calagiu, Miriam Constantin, Edith Olosz, Veronica Vaida, Andrada Simion, Dragos Cordos, Levent Sag, Florenz Schneider, and Jesper Vaarwerk.

Claim your Gift

I wrote, edited, and designed the material from this book by myself. Except for the cover, I took care of the entire process from start to finish. I felt like an artisan; you indeed derive immense pleasure from your craft when you're a generalist. Yet, the risk is clear: I probably made some (many?) mistakes. I checked for typos and other (grammatical) errors quite a few times already and every time I checked again, I found new errors. If you spot a typo or any kind of (grammatical) mistake, send me an email at <u>sovereignartist@outlook.com</u> letting me know what and where that mistake is so I can fix it. As a small gift, you will get FREE access to my favorite workshop: *Sipping Wine with Da Vinci*